Community Helpers

Veterinarians

by Dee Ready

Reading Consultant:
Dr. Sheldon Rubin
American Veterinary Medical Association
Public Relations Council

Bridgestone Books

an Imprint of Capstone Press

Bridgestone Books are published by Capstone Press
151 Good Counsel Drive, P.O. Box 669, Mankato, Minnesota 56002
http://www.capstone-press.com

Library of Congress Cataloging-in-Publication Data
Ready, Dee.
    Veterinarians/by Dee Ready.
    p. cm.—(Community helpers)
    Includes bibliographical references (p. 24) and index.
    Summary: Explains the clothing, tools, schooling, and work of veterinarians.
    ISBN 1-56065-514-3
    1. Veterinarian Medicine—Juvenile literature. 2. Veterinary Medicine—
    Vocational guidance—Juvenile literature. [1. Veterinarians. 2. Veterinary
    Medicine. 3. Occupations.] I. Title. II. Series: Community helpers
    (Mankato, Minn.)
SF756.R43   1997
636.089'06952—dc21   96-47312
                                                                        CIP
                                                                        AC

Photo credits
Faith Uridel, cover
FPG/James Levin, 4; Jonathan Meyers, 6; Stephen Simpson, 8; USDA, 10;
    Jerry Driendl, 12
James Rowan, 18
Michelle Mero Riedel, 16, 20
Unicorn/Alon Reninger, 14

2 3 4 5 6 04 03 02 01 00

Table of Contents

Veterinarians

Veterinarians are animal doctors. They are also called vets. Vets care for sick animals. They help healthy animals stay that way.

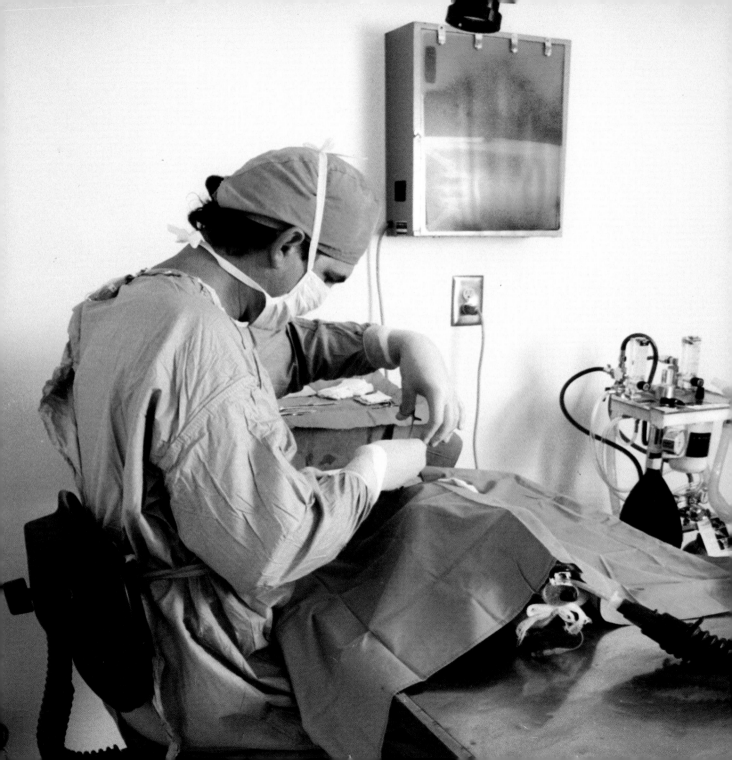

What Veterinarians Do

Veterinarians try to make sick animals better. Sometimes vets must operate to help a sick animal. They also set broken bones. Vets sometimes give shots to animals.

Different Kinds of Veterinarians

There are different kinds of veterinarians for different animals. About half of all vets take care of pets. Other vets help farm animals and horses. Some vets work at the zoo.

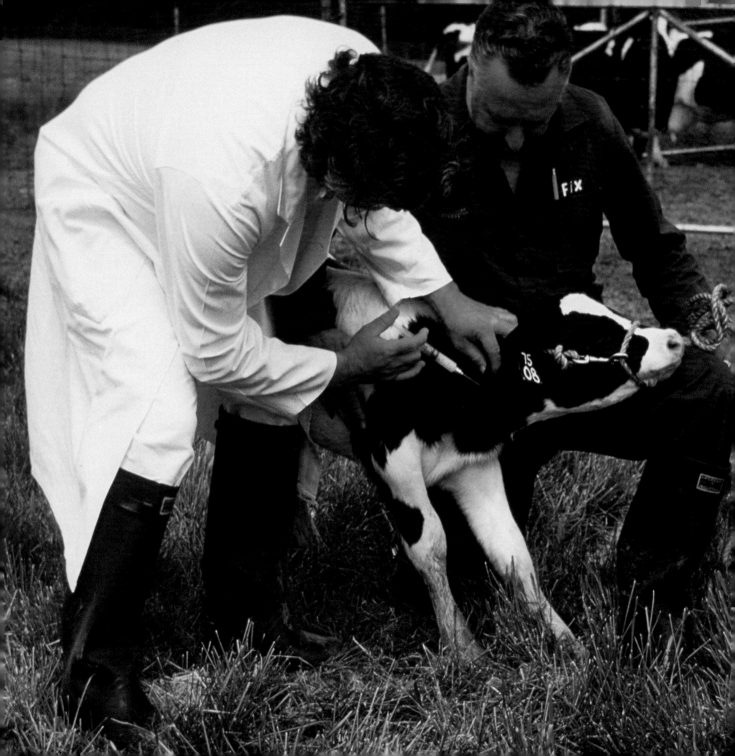

What Veterinarians Wear

Veterinarians who work in an office usually wear lab coats. Vets who work on a farm wear tall, rubber boots and coveralls. A coverall is a one-piece suit worn over clothes to keep them clean.

Tools Veterinarians Use

Veterinarians use the same type of tools as human doctors. But a vet's tools are made just for animals. Vets use a stethoscope to listen to an animal's heartbeat. They use a syringe to give shots.

Veterinarians and School

Veterinarians must have at least two years of college. Then they go to veterinarian school. Vet school lasts for four years. After they finish school, students must pass a state exam to be vets.

Where Veterinarians Work

Most veterinarians work at animal hospitals. Animal hospitals have examining rooms and operating rooms. There are also places for sick pets to stay. Farm vets go to the home of the sick animal.

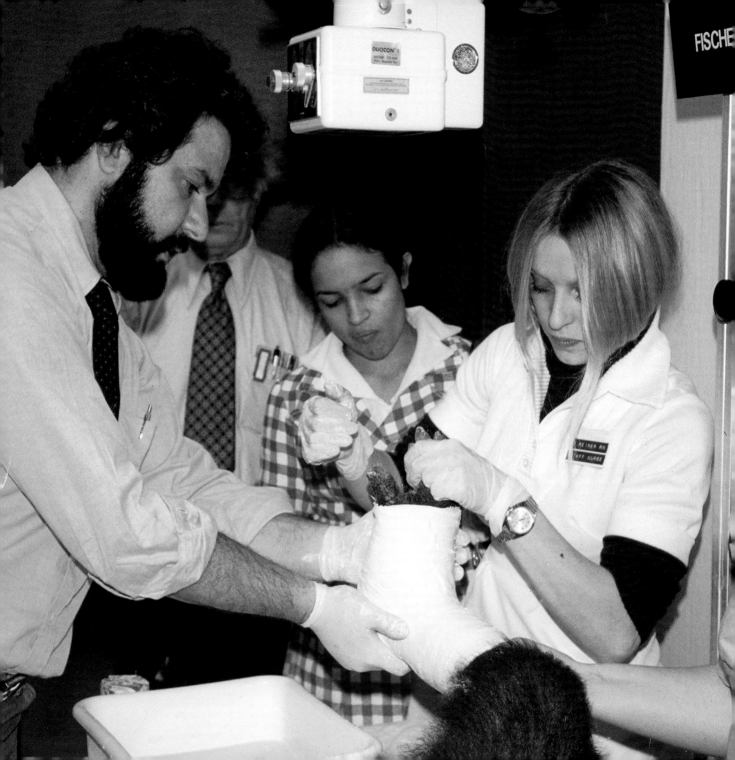

People Who Help Veterinarians

Veterinarians need help with their work. A receptionist answers calls for office visits. An assistant helps the vet operate. Often the pet owner or farmer helps the vet, too.

Veterinarians Help Others

Veterinarians help both animals and people. They take care of people's pets. Sometimes they help farm animals have babies. They show people how to care for their animals.

Hands On: Care for Birds

A veterinarian's job is to care for animals. You can care for animals that come to your own backyard.

Birds are everywhere. They need people to care for them. Here are some ways you can care for the birds.

1. Leave birdseed out on your porch or window. This will keep your birds fed.
2. Make a birdbath. Birds like to clean themselves in a bath. Leave some clean water in a pie plate for them.
3. Get a birdhouse. You can buy a birdhouse at a store. Or you can build one of your own. A birdhouse gives the birds a safe place to live.

Words to Know

community (kuh-MEW-nuh-tee)—a group of people living in the same area

examine (eg-ZAM-uhn)—to look over closely

lab coat (LAHB KOHT)—a long cotton coat that covers the clothing

operate (AHP-uh-rate)—to cut open a body to fix a medical problem

stethoscope (STETH-uh-skope)—a medical tool used to listen to the sounds of the chest

syringe (suh-RINJ)—a tube with a plunger and a hollow needle used to give shots

Read More

Bowman-Kruhm, Mary. *A Day in the Life of a Veterinarian.* The Kids' Career Library. New York: PowerKids Press, 1999.
Flanagan, Alice K. *Dr. Friedman Helps Animals.* Our Neighborhood. New York: Children's Press, 1999.
Schomp, Virginia. *If You Were a Veterinarian.* New York: Benchmark Books, 1998.

Internet Sites

Acmepet
http://www.acmepet.com/
Kid's Korner
http://www.avma.org/care4pets/avmakids.htm